JAPANESE AMERICAN
INTERNMENT

BY MICHAEL BURGAN

COMPASS POINT BOOKS
a capstone imprint

Compass Point Books are published by Capstone,
1710 Roe Crest Drive, North Mankato, Minnesota 56003
www.mycapstone.com

Editorial Credits

Sarah Bennett, Jaclyn Jaycox, Angela Kaelberer, Kelli Lageson,
Kathy McColley, and Catherine Neitge

Photo Credits

AP Photo: Dennis Cook, 97, 98; DVIC/NARA: cover; Getty Images: Bettmann,
12, 14, 35, 65, 78, 88, Keystone, 24; Library of Congress: 38, 58, 62, 66, 70,
102 (right); National Archives and Records Administration: 10, 29, 32, 39, 42,
46, 47, 49, 51, 54, 60, 73, 75, 82, 93, 101 (left), 102 (left); Newscom: Everett
Collection, 43, 44, UIG Universal Images Group/Underwood Archives, 23,
ZUMA Press/Ron Sachs, 31; Shutterstock: Everett Historical, 2, 6, 16, 52,
85, 100, Hank Shiffman, 94, Rena Schild, 103; U.S. Army, 101 (right); XNR
Productions, 56

Library of Congress Cataloging-in-Publication Data

Names: Burgan, Michael, author.
Title: Japanese American internment / by Michael Burgan.
Description: North Mankato, Minnesota : Compass Point Books, a Capstone
imprint, [2018] | Series: Eyewitness to World War II | Includes bibliographical
references and index. | Audience: Grades 4-6. | Audience: Ages 10-12.
Identifiers: LCCN 2017010250 | ISBN 9780756555818 (library binding) |
ISBN 9780756555856 (paperback) | ISBN 9780756555856 (ebook pdf)
Subjects: LCSH: Japanese Americans—Evacuation and relocation, 1942–
1945—Juvenile literature. | World War, 1939-1945—Japanese Americans—
Juvenile literature. | Japanese—United States—History—Juvenile literature.
Classification: LCC D769.8.A6 B843 2018 | DDC 940.53/1773089956—dc23
LC record available at https://lccn.loc.gov/2017010250

Printed and bound in the USA.
010368F17

CONTENTS

The USS *California* was just one of the many U.S. battleships damaged or destroyed by the Japanese during the attack on Pearl Harbor.

CHAPTER ONE

PRISONERS IN THEIR OWN COUNTRY

It was December 7, 1941. Seven-year-old Jeanne Wakatsuki waved as she watched her father's fishing boat sail away from the wharf in Long Beach, California. Her father, Ko, and older brothers, Woody and Bill, were heading out to catch the sardines that they sold to the local canneries.

The Wakatsuki family's boat, along with about 25 others sailing out that day, wasn't expected to return for several days or even weeks, depending on how well the fishing went. That day, however, the boats turned around almost immediately and returned to the wharf. Jeanne and her family soon learned why. That morning Japanese planes and submarines had attacked the Pearl Harbor Naval Base in Hawaii, killing more than 2,400

Americans. The United States declared war on Japan the next day, joining the many other countries that were fighting World War II.

Ko Wakatsuki had immigrated to Hawaii from Japan in 1904 at age 17 and later settled in California. He and his wife, Riku, had 10 children, all of whom were born in the United States and were American citizens. But U.S. laws prevented Japanese immigrants such as Ko and Riku from becoming American citizens.

Immediately after the Pearl Harbor attack, many Japanese immigrants were questioned about their loyalty to the United States. Some were arrested and accused of providing aid to Japan. Ko was one of them. He was charged with delivering oil to Japanese submarines—a charge he denied—and was sent to a men's prison camp at Fort Lincoln in Bismarck, North Dakota.

Riku, her mother, and her four children still living at home left their home in Ocean Park, California. They first moved into her son Woody's home in Terminal Island and then to Los Angeles. They were living there on February 19, 1942, when President Franklin D. Roosevelt signed Executive Order 9066. The order allowed the government to round up people of Japanese descent who were living on the West Coast and send them to what were called relocation camps. Many Americans were worried that the Japanese Americans would sympathize with Japan and work to help it win the war, possibly by spying for Japan or sabotaging American factories and military operations.

In March 1942, Jeanne and her mother, grandmother, four brothers, two sisters, two sisters-in-law, and a baby niece boarded a bus in Los Angeles. They traveled all day until reaching Owens Valley near the Nevada

JAPANESE AMERICANS

During World War II, people of Japanese ancestry were classified according to how long they had lived in the United States. Those who were born in Japan were called *Issei*. Their children who were born in the United States were called *Nisei*. Most Nisei were born before World War II. The grandchildren of the Issei, known as the *Sansei*, were mostly born during or after World War II. Some Japanese Americans born in the United States went to Japan for school and then returned to the United States. They were called *Kibei*.

border. It was a dusty, barren area consisting of hastily built wooden barracks surrounded by barbed wire and guard towers. Its name was Manzanar War Relocation Center, and it was one of 10 internment camps that housed Japanese Americans during World War II.

More than 10,000 Japanese Americans were crowded into 504 barracks at Manzanar War Relocation Center.

Jeanne and her family—her father joined them after nine months in the prison camp—spent the next three years at the camp. They were not allowed to leave even though they had done nothing wrong. They were among nearly 120,000 people of Japanese ancestry who were imprisoned during World War II. More than half of them were American citizens.

Many Americans who supported the internment genuinely feared a Japanese invasion of the United States, either in Hawaii or on the West Coast of the United States. At the time most people of Japanese ancestry lived in the western United States, with the largest concentration in California, Oregon, and Washington. Some U.S. leaders worried that people of Japanese ancestry—even those who were U.S. citizens—would be disloyal to the United States. They believed that sending Japanese Americans to the camps, where their actions could be watched and limited, was needed to protect national security.

Racism also played a large role in the internment of Japanese Americans. Fear and hatred of the Japanese

The bombing of Pearl Harbor only fueled racism and prejudice against the Japanese. Anti-Japanese signs were a common sight after the attack.

and other non-Caucasians in the United States had been around long before World War II. Anyone who was born in a country at war with the United States was considered an enemy alien. In the days after the attack on Pearl Harbor, Germany and Italy also declared war on the United States. Nearly a million people from those two nations living in the United States became enemy aliens as well. Although some were considered threats to

U.S. security and were forced to move, only about 15,000 were sent to internment camps. But unlike the Japanese, the Italians and Germans were Caucasians. They didn't face the same kind of prejudice the Japanese did.

The last Japanese Americans left the camps in 1946, more than six months after World War II ended. The years in the camps changed their lives forever. They also raised questions about the actions a nation should take during wartime—questions still debated today.

About 10,000 Chinese workers were brought in to work on the transcontinental railroad. They lived in makeshift camps right along the railroad.

CHAPTER TWO

JAPANESE IMMIGRATION

The Japanese weren't the first Asian people to immigrate to the United States. Beginning in 1850, many Chinese men came to the United States to work in California gold mines. When the Gold Rush ended, many of them stayed in the United States. They were willing to perform dangerous jobs and work for lower wages than American citizens expected. In the 1860s Chinese workers played an important part in completing the transcontinental railroad between Omaha, Nebraska, and Sacramento, California. They also worked in laundries, on farms, and as servants. Some saved enough money to establish their own businesses and bring their families to the United States.

In the 1870s, though, the United States had an economic slowdown. There was more competition for the fewer jobs that were available, and many Americans began to resent the Chinese immigrants because they would work for less. Congress in 1882 passed the Chinese Exclusion Act, which prohibited immigration of Chinese laborers for 10 years. It was the first U.S. law designed to keep immigrants out of a country. The Geary Act in 1892 extended the immigration ban for another 10 years.

Japan's leaders had closed their country to trade with western nations and visitors from them about 1600. Japan remained isolated from the West until 1853,

The Chinese Exclusion Act was approved on May 6, 1882.

when U.S. Navy Commodore Matthew C. Perry traveled to Japan. On his second visit in 1854, Perry negotiated a treaty that allowed trade between Japan and the United States. This relationship eventually speeded immigration of Japanese people to the West. American businessman Eugene Van Reed brought about 200 Japanese people to the South Pacific islands of Hawaii and Guam in 1868 to work on sugarcane plantations there. Hawaii was then an independent kingdom, and Guam was a Spanish colony. Both islands became U.S. territories in 1898.

The first Japanese immigrants came to the United States in 1869. With the help of a Dutch businessman, about 20 Japanese came to Gold Hill, California, to farm and produce silk. But the Gold Hill settlement soon failed because of lack of water and money. Within about a year, the Japanese immigrants had moved elsewhere in California.

Because Chinese people were barred entry by the Chinese Exclusion Act, the nation had too few workers to do the kinds of jobs the Chinese did. An increasing number of Japanese immigrants began to fill those jobs.

About 27,000 came to the United States from 1891 to 1900, and almost 130,000 arrived in the next decade. More than 75 percent of Japanese immigrants settled in California, Oregon, and Washington, with California having the most.

Early Japanese immigrants worked in mines and canning factories, as well as on railroad crews. Over time, most turned to agriculture, especially in sunny California. Although their first jobs were usually working for American farmers, many Issei saved money and bought their own land. They started some of the most productive farms in the state. Although they owned just 1 percent of California farmland, Japanese Americans produced 10 percent of the crops grown there. Other Japanese immigrants opened successful businesses.

By 1900 some Americans were associating the Japanese with the Chinese. Both groups were Asian. Both came from countries with emperors, and both followed religions other than Christianity. Like what happened with the Chinese, the growing number of

Japanese immigrants and their economic success angered some people in the western United States. The feelings against the Japanese often resulted in racism. Japanese students in San Francisco, California, weren't allowed to attend schools with white students in 1906. Mobs of angry Americans sometimes attacked Japanese workers.

Leaders in Japan were upset by what was happening to the Japanese immigrants in the United States. The officials asked President Theodore Roosevelt to investigate the situation in California.

Roosevelt struck a deal with Japan in February 1907 called the Gentleman's Agreement. The president met with San Francisco Mayor Eugene Schmitz and the city school board. The board agreed to allow

GENTLEMAN'S AGREEMENT

The 1907 agreement between Japan and the United States was known as a gentleman's agreement because instead of a formal treaty, it was simply an informal agreement. Such agreements were common in business and trade relations in the early part of the 20th century. The agreements could not be enforced in a court of law, but they were effective as long as the two parties both kept their word.

Japanese students to return to the city's public schools. In return, the Japanese government agreed to stop issuing passports to Japanese workers who wanted to go to the United States. Japan had enacted a similar rule in 1900, but workers found a way around it by going to Hawaii, Canada, or Mexico before entering the United States. The Gentleman's Agreement with Japan let the United States refuse entry to Japanese immigrants who held passports issued by other territories or countries. Roosevelt also promised Japan that the United States wouldn't completely cut off Japanese immigration.

As Roosevelt had hoped, the agreement eased the tension in diplomatic relations between Japan and the United States. It also reduced the number of Japanese immigrants. But it didn't end racism and discrimination toward the immigrants.

Mary Tsukamoto was born in San Francisco in 1915 and moved with her family at age 10 to the small town of Florin, California. Florin had a Japanese population of about 2,500 people. Many worked on the nearby farms or in factories in town. Mary's father raised strawberries

ALIEN LAND LAWS

The California legislature passed the Alien Land Law in 1913. It was based on another U.S. law that prevented Japanese Americans from becoming naturalized U.S. citizens. The Alien Land Law said that "aliens ineligible for citizenship"—meaning the Issei— could not own land in California. Japanese businessman Takao Ozawa challenged the law barring the naturalization of Japanese aliens in 1916. Ozawa's case went to the U.S. Supreme Court, which upheld the ban in 1923.

Other western states, including New Mexico, Oregon, Idaho, Washington, and Montana, passed alien land laws similar to California's in the 1920s. But some Issei could buy or hold land in the names of their Nisei children. Since the Nisei were born in the United States, they had automatically become U.S. citizens. A second California land law passed in 1920 made it harder for the Issei to use this loophole. Japanese citizens who wanted to buy land had to prove that they were not buying it for someone else. The state could also seize any land that had been bought by Nisei with their parents' money.

The alien land laws in California were enforced until 1952. That year, the California Supreme Court ruled that the laws violated the 14th Amendment to the U.S. Constitution, which guarantees the rights of U.S. citizens. The California legislature didn't formally remove the law until 1956.

and grapes and earned a good living, although he wasn't allowed to own land because he was a Japanese immigrant. Only Japanese children could attend Mary's elementary school in Florin, but she went to the town's high school with children of other races. Mary said later that although farmers in Florin were happy to hire Japanese workers, many other white people there weren't pleased. "The Native Sons and Daughters and the American Legion and the California Federation of Labor and the Hearst papers and the McClatchy papers all claimed that the Japanese were going to own all of California, that we were going to take over the land," she said. "So many people decided that they wanted to try to get us out."

Congress passed the Immigration Act in 1924, which restricted the number of immigrants generally. The maximum number of immigrants to be allowed each year from a country would be equal to 2 percent of the total number from that country who were in the United States in 1890. The law also excluded people who were not eligible to become citizens. Since there were

The Nisei quickly adapted to the American way of life. They considered themselves Japanese Americans, not just Japanese living in the United States.

few Japanese immigrants in the United States in 1890, and previous laws had not allowed the Issei to become citizens, almost all immigration from Japan ended. But as the Nisei married and had families of their own, the Japanese American population continued to grow. By 1930, nearly 140,000 people of Japanese descent lived in the United States. Nearly 90 percent of them lived on the West Coast.

Japanese troops invaded Manchuria, China, in 1931.

CHAPTER THREE

TENSIONS WITH JAPAN

While Japanese immigrants were facing racism and persecution in the United States, Japan's relationship with the United States and other western countries was deteriorating. Japan was eager to expand its empire by taking over countries and territories that were rich in natural resources that Japan lacked, such as metal deposits and oil.

Japan invaded Manchuria, a region of China, in 1931. China was much larger than Japan, but was in turmoil because of a civil war. By the next year, Japan had established a puppet government in Manchuria. Chinese officials ran the government under Japan's orders.

Franklin D. Roosevelt—a distant cousin of Theodore Roosevelt—was elected U.S. president in 1932. Roosevelt's family had once had strong business ties with China, and Roosevelt worried about Japan's aggression toward China. He also viewed Japan as an American rival for dominance in the Pacific. In addition to Hawaii, the United States controlled the Philippines and several small Pacific islands. Japanese leaders were considering the possibility of someday having to fight a war with the United States. Joseph Grew, the U.S. ambassador to Japan, told Roosevelt, "The Japanese fighting forces consider the United States as their potential enemy."

Japan continued to show force against China. By 1937 the two countries were at war. During the Second Sino-Japanese War (1937–1945), Japanese soldiers tortured and murdered more than 250,000 Chinese people in the Nanking region alone. U.S. leaders were upset by Japan's actions and supported China in the war with both money and military supplies. The U.S. government also cut off sales to Japan of oil and other raw materials that could be used in the war. Both actions increased the Japanese leaders' anger toward Americans.

JAPANESE ESPIONAGE

President Franklin D. Roosevelt in 1934 ordered a study of possible Japanese espionage on the West Coast. For the rest of the decade, government agents continued to look for suspicious activity among Japanese Americans and Japanese aliens living in the United States. Even before the attack on Pearl Harbor, Roosevelt had ordered his aides to conduct a new study on the loyalty of Japanese Americans. He wanted to know which country they would support if there were a war between Japan and the United States. The report said about the Nisei:

"We do not want to throw a lot of American citizens into a concentration camp, of course, and especially as the almost unanimous verdict is that in the case of war they will be very, very quiet. . . . Because in addition to being quite contented with the American way of life, they know they are 'in a spot.'"

The report concluded that most Japanese Americans would try hard to prove their loyalty and would ignore racist treatment by white Americans. Yet the report also said some Japanese Americans might spy for Japan or carry out sabotage.

While Japan was trying to expand its empire in the Pacific, Germany and its leader, Adolf Hitler, were planning to take over Europe. German troops invaded Poland on September 1, 1939, which started World War II. Germany continued its march through Europe during 1939 and 1940, conquering the Netherlands, Belgium, and France. Japan, Italy, and Germany signed the Tripartite Pact, forming the Axis Alliance, on September 27, 1940. The Axis powers' main rival was Great Britain, the leader of the Allied forces. The United States was supporting the Allies with aid, but most Americans strongly opposed getting involved in the war. Great Britain was desperate for help from the United States. Germany was carrying out bombing attacks on British cities, and Japanese troops were threatening British colonies in the Pacific Ocean.

American and Japanese diplomats were still trying to negotiate a peaceful settlement of the conflicts between the two countries in the fall of 1941. But after the U.S. government broke the secret code Japan used when sending messages to its diplomats in the United States,

President Roosevelt learned that the Japanese were also preparing to fight the United States.

Roosevelt and his advisers thought the Japanese probably would attack, but they didn't know where. They thought the most likely targets were U.S. bases in the Philippines or Guam or British bases in Asia. An attack on Hawaii was possible, but U.S. Navy leaders there didn't think that would happen. Japan and Hawaii are 3,850 miles (6,196 kilometers) apart. In those days, that was considered an enormous distance to travel and could not be done without refueling ships. It would also be very difficult for a large strike force to travel that far without being detected.

As Roosevelt and his advisers had expected, the Japanese did attack, but exactly where they hadn't expected. Early in the morning of December 7, 1941, the Japanese launched a

The USS *West Virginia* sank after being bombed by the Japanese.

29

surprise attack on Pearl Harbor Naval Base on the island of Oahu, Hawaii. For two hours, Japanese planes and submarines attacked U.S. warships docked or anchored in the harbor. They also destroyed airplanes parked on airfields. When the smoke lifted, 21 U.S. ships had been either sunk or damaged, 188 aircraft had been destroyed, and another 159 airplanes had been damaged. More than 2,400 Americans—mostly soldiers or sailors, but also some civilians—were killed. Nearly 1,000 others were wounded.

That morning 17-year-old Japanese American Daniel Inouye walked out of his family's home in Honolulu, not far from Pearl Harbor, and saw Japanese bombers flying. He later remembered thinking:

"What would become of the [Japanese Americans] . . . suddenly rendered so vulnerable and helpless by this monstrous betrayal at the hands of [Japan]? . . . I, too, had been betrayed, and all of my family."

Inouye didn't know what would happen to him or his family. But he knew that their lives had changed forever.

FROM PEARL HARBOR TO SENATE SUCCESS

Daniel Inouye was born to Japanese parents on September 7, 1924, in Honolulu, Hawaii. Like most Japanese Americans in Hawaii, he and his family weren't sent to the internment camps.

Inouye volunteered for the U.S. Army in 1943, serving in a Japanese American regiment. His right arm was destroyed during a battle, and he received medals, including the Bronze Star, two Purple Hearts, and the Medal of Honor, for his bravery during the war.

Inouye served in Hawaii's territorial legislature during the 1950s. When Hawaii became a state in 1959, he became its first member of the House of Representatives. He was elected to the U.S. Senate in 1962 and served in the Senate until his death in 2012 at age 88.

Japanese Americans waved to their friends and neighbors as they departed for one of the assembly centers.

CHAPTER FOUR

LIVING UNDER SUSPICION

After the attack on Pearl Harbor, Japanese Americans found themselves under a great deal of suspicion. The Justice Department immediately approved the arrests of 1,500 Issei living in the United States. Among them were many leaders of Japanese cultural and religious organizations. The government thought they were a threat because of their presumed loyalty to Japan. Others, like Jeanne Wakatsuki's father, were business owners suspected of providing supplies or financial aid to Japan's military. Many of the Issei arrested were sent to internment camps in Montana, New Mexico, and North Dakota.

Other steps taken against Issei after December 7 included restricting their travel and freezing their bank accounts. Blocking access to their accounts was a great hardship for them, because they couldn't withdraw their money to pay bills or even to buy food.

Rumors began to quickly spread through the United States about a supposed Japanese American threat. Newspapers reported that Japanese planes were seen flying over the West Coast, and civilian boats were said to be flashing messages to Japanese warships at sea. Even some military officers spread rumors, warning that the Japanese would soon attack the mainland. But all of the rumors were false, as were reports that Japanese Americans in Hawaii had acted as spies for Japan. Even so, in Hawaii the government established martial law. The military took control of the local police and government to help prevent any spying or sabotage by disloyal Japanese Americans.

The U.S. military had organized the country into four defense command zones in March 1941—Western, Eastern, Central, and Southern—to guard against and prepare for enemy attack. The Western Defense Command included California, Oregon, Washington,

Arizona, Montana, Utah, Nevada, and Idaho. Its headquarters was in San Francisco, and its leader was Lieutenant General John DeWitt.

John DeWitt feared the Japanese living in the United States would be disloyal and aid Japan during the war.

After the December 7 attack, DeWitt called for moving all Issei age 14 and over from the West Coast. At the time, DeWitt didn't believe it was legal to send the Nisei to internment camps. But other government officials disagreed. U.S. Representative Leland Ford of California said, "All Japanese, whether citizen or not . . . [should be] placed in inland concentration camps." More lawmakers in the West began to accept this idea, as did some California farmers. The farmers saw internment as an opportunity to gain control of land that the Japanese owned. As the weeks passed, the calls for action against the Japanese Americans grew in number.

President Roosevelt was aware of the situation with the Japanese Americans, but it wasn't his top priority.

He was more concerned with preparing the country to fight against the Axis powers. He relied on government lawyers, military officers, and legislators to make plans for dealing with the Japanese in the United States.

At first Roosevelt listened to aides and government officials who said most Japanese Americans would remain loyal to the United States. Treasury Secretary Henry Morgenthau Jr. said the government should not be "suddenly mopping up 150,000 Japanese and putting them behind barbed wire." Yet the president refused to make a public statement saying that the Nisei and most Issei were not a danger to the country. If he had issued such a statement, it may have calmed Americans' fears about the supposed threat that their Japanese neighbors posed to the country.

Navy Secretary Frank Knox and other military officials were worried about the Japanese Americans in Hawaii. Knox supported interning them, either on one of Hawaii's islands or on the mainland. But the military officials in Hawaii opposed this idea. The 150,000 Japanese Americans in Hawaii formed about one-third

A VOLUNTARY RELOCATION

Before President Roosevelt issued Executive Order 9066, several thousand Japanese Americans took action to keep their freedoms. After the Pearl Harbor attack, they left the West Coast and moved inland to states such as Nevada. They thought that they would have a better chance of being left alone in those areas. But that didn't happen. Some were even met at state borders by armed citizens who refused to allow them to enter.

A government report said some Japanese Americans were thrown into jail for no reason, and "many were greeted by 'No Japs Wanted' signs on the main streets of [inland] communities."

Most of the Japanese Americans who headed east quickly returned to their homes and families on the West Coast. Within weeks, they would be moving again—but this time, they didn't have a choice of where to go.

of the territory's population. If they were suddenly removed, the islands would take a huge economic hit. The pineapple and sugar plantation owners didn't want to lose the workers they depended on to tend their fields. And fewer people would be available to help rebuild

Pearl Harbor and do other important work. About 1,500
Japanese in Hawaii were eventually arrested. Many of
them were involved in groups with direct ties to Japan.
The rest remained free.

In California, General DeWitt was preparing to
remove Issei from areas near military bases or defense
plants in the state. He said he expected "a violent
outburst of coordinated and controlled sabotage" by
Japanese Americans. Even though no sabotage had
happened, DeWitt believed the disloyal Japanese
Americans were simply waiting for their orders to

Japanese American detainees at the Pinedale Assembly Center waited for
transportation to a relocation center.

People of Japanese ancestry were jammed into trucks with their belongings while being relocated to the Santa Anita Assembly Center in Arcadia, California.

strike. He and other top government officials, including California Attorney General Earl Warren, were now supporting internment for all Japanese Americans. They believed there was no way to tell a disloyal Japanese American from a loyal one. The only way to keep the country safe, they said, was to lock them all up.

By mid-February 1942, Japan had won several major battles in the Pacific, which increased white Americans' fear of a Japanese invasion. The pressure to take action against the Japanese Americans was too much for Roosevelt to ignore. He issued Executive Order 9066 on February 19, 1942. The presidential order gave the military the power to list areas of the country "from which any or all persons may be excluded." Roosevelt's order didn't mention any particular group of people, but the military and civilian officials who would carry

THE FIRST EVACUEES

Some Japanese Americans were forced to leave their homes before President Roosevelt's executive order was issued. They were mainly fishermen's families who lived on Terminal Island, which is in San Pedro Harbor near Long Beach, California. The U.S. Navy owned the small island, which was home to a navy base, two shipyards, and some fish canneries that employed Japanese Americans. Immediately after the Pearl Harbor attack, most of the fishermen were arrested and their boats and radios confiscated to prevent their being used to aid Japan.

In late January 1941 Navy Secretary Frank Knox told the Japanese American women, children, and old people left on the island that they would have several weeks to prepare to leave their homes. But that wasn't true. The residents were told on February 25 that they would be moved in less than 48 hours. They scrambled

out the plan knew that Japanese Americans were the target. Rumors of mass evacuation swept through Japanese American neighborhoods, but no one could give the residents a definite answer. They could only wait anxiously for an unknown future.

to pack needed items and prized possessions, since they could take only what they could carry with them.

After the evacuation order went out, dealers in secondhand property descended on the island, offering to buy the evacuees' furniture, appliances, and other personal property, usually for much less than they were worth. Jeanne Wakatsuki later recalled a dealer trying to buy a 12-piece set of antique Japanese porcelain dishes from her mother. The set was worth at least $200, but the dealer offered $15. When Mrs. Wakatsuki refused, the man said he could possibly pay $17.50. At that point, Jeanne's mother had enough. She grabbed a plate and hurled it to the ground at the dealer's feet. He protested that she shouldn't destroy the valuable dishes, then turned and ran from the house. "When he was gone," Jeanne said later, "she stood there smashing cups and bowls and platters until the whole set lay in scattered blue and white fragments across the wooden floor."

Men, women, and children of Japanese ancestry were forced to go to assembly centers, leaving behind everything except the items they could carry.

CHAPTER FIVE

FORCED OUT

First there were the signs. In late March 1942, signs written in English were posted on telephone poles and in store windows in Japanese American neighborhoods across California, as well as in areas of Oregon, Washington, and Arizona. The signs told Japanese Americans to go to one of 16 "assembly centers." All of the areas were in California except for one each in Arizona, Washington, and Oregon. If the Japanese Americans refused to go to the centers voluntarily, the signs said, they would be removed by force.

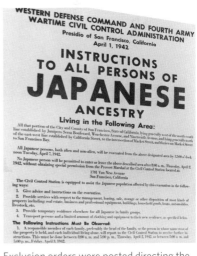

Exclusion orders were posted directing the removal of all people of Japanese ancestry.

Like the evacuees at Terminal Island, these evacuees could only bring what they could carry, including necessary items such as clothing, dishes, sheets, and towels. Many families held yard sales to sell the items they couldn't bring. Others sent their belongings to warehouses, where the government said it would store the goods. Pets had to be left with friends and neighbors or simply abandoned, along with any personal property that couldn't be sold.

Evacuees had little notice and many sold their businesses for a fraction of their worth.

Many Japanese Americans owned their own homes and businesses. They either had to sell them at a great loss or lock them up and leave them empty, hoping for the best. One family owned an ice cream shop containing $8,000 in equipment and $10,000 in supplies and inventory. "Well, we had people coming in droves offering us a hundred dollars, two hundred dollars," the owner said later, "and finally this man offered us a thousand dollars. We put him on hold for a couple of days, but we took it the day before we left."

Japanese Americans who owned farmland also faced a dilemma when they were evacuated. Some found help from white neighbors and friends. The Hiyama family of Fowler, California, asked Kamm Oliver to look after their vineyard while they were gone. Oliver said later that it was "the right thing to do," even though some white people called him a traitor. Oliver cared for the vineyards

JAPANESE CANADIANS

While the U.S. government was debating what to do with the Issei and Nisei, Canada took steps against its Japanese residents. As in the United States, most people of Japanese descent in Canada lived on the West Coast. The Canadian government began making plans on January 14, 1942, to intern Japanese men between the ages of 18 and 45. Eventually, entire families were sent to what the government called protective areas. In the end, about 21,000 people of Japanese ancestry were sent to the camps. More than half were Canadian citizens. As in the United States, racism and fear fueled the decision to force the Japanese Canadians from their homes.

Japanese Americans wore identification tags to help ensure families stayed intact during all phases of the evacuation.

and each year sent the Hiyamas a check at their camp for the sale of the raisins made from their grapes. But many other Japanese Americans found that their land had been taken from them and sold to others.

General DeWitt's plan divided the West Coast into two zones. No Japanese Americans could live in the Prohibited Zone, which extended the length of the Pacific Coast through Washington, Oregon, and California and

along part of the Mexican border. Farther inland was
the Restricted Zone, where Japanese Americans would
have limited freedom to live and work. A new federal
law prohibited anyone from refusing to leave a military
exclusion area, such as the Prohibited Zone.

At the end of March 1942, the first evacuation in
the Prohibited Zone took place on Bainbridge Island in
Washington. California evacuations quickly followed.

Japanese Americans arrived at the Santa Anita Assembly Center in April 1942.

Most of the evacuees went willingly and quietly. The military didn't have to use force. Many Japanese American leaders urged their fellow Japanese Americans

PROTESTING RELOCATION

One of the few Japanese Americans who spoke out against relocation was journalist James Omura, a Nisei who lived in California and had worked for Japanese-language newspapers. He protested the relocation to members of Congress in February 1942. "Are we to be condemned merely on the basis of our racial origin?" he asked them. "Is citizenship such a light and transient thing that that which is our inalienable right in normal times can be torn from us in times of war?"

Omura moved to Denver, Colorado, along with about 5,000 other Nisei in late March 1942. Few Japanese Americans lived in Denver, and the city was far from the West Coast, where a Japanese invasion seemed most likely. So the Japanese Americans in Denver weren't considered a threat and forced into camps. Omura served as the English-language editor at the *Rocky Shimpo*, a Japanese American newspaper in Denver.

Omura was arrested in 1944 and charged with conspiring to help people avoid the military draft. He was found not guilty when the case went to trial in Wyoming.

to cooperate with the government. Going voluntarily, they thought, would show their loyalty to the United States.

Most of the assembly centers were located at sites such as racetracks and fairgrounds. They were chosen because they were usually on large areas of land that already had buildings. But the buildings had housed horses and farm animals. Entire families lived in stalls built to hold one or two horses. Internee Ernest Uno later remembered: "Those stables just reeked. There was nothing you could do. The amount of lye they threw on it to clear the odor

Converted horse stalls were used as family apartments. Some lived there for several months before being moved to relocation centers.

and stuff, it didn't help. It still reeked of urine and horse manure. It was so degrading for people to live in those conditions."

College student Yoshiko Uchida was assigned to the Tanforan Assembly Center near San Bruno, California, with her mother and older sister. The FBI had arrested her father and sent him to a camp in Missoula, Montana.

Uchida's family lived in a stable with 25 other families. The stalls were separated from each other by wooden partitions that were too low to provide much privacy. The internees brought their own dishes and silverware to eat meals prepared in large mess halls. There was one latrine for men and one for women, each having eight showers and eight toilets. People often stood in long lines waiting for a chance to wash or use the toilet. They also stood in line to wash clothes, linens, and diapers in the tubs in the laundry barracks. "The hot water was often gone by 9 a.m.," Uchida said later, "and many women got up at 3:00 and 4:00 in the morning to do their wash, all of which, including sheets, had to be done entirely by hand."

Evacuees had to wait in long lines at the mess hall for breakfast, lunch, and dinner.

The assembly center was just a temporary stop for the Uchida family. The government kept Japanese Americans in the centers until the relocation centers were completed. The Uchidas stayed at Tanforan for a little more than three months. Then they were taken to Topaz, a camp in Utah. By this time, Mr. Uchida had been allowed to join his family.

President Roosevelt on March 18 signed Executive Order 9102, which created the War Relocation Authority (WRA). This civilian agency was put in charge of the internment camps.

Future U.S. President Dwight D. Eisenhower's brother Milton, who was the first head of the WRA, chose the sites for the 10 relocation camps. Eight were in isolated areas of the West—Tule Lake and Manzanar, California; Minidoka, Idaho; Poston and Gila River, Arizona; Heart Mountain, Wyoming; Topaz, Utah; and Granada, Colorado. The other two camps, Jerome and Rohwer, were in Arkansas. The camps were built far from roads and railways, so if any of the internees escaped, they would have trouble reaching a town.

Manzanar was the first camp to open, on March 21, 1942. The others opened during the next seven months, with the final camp, Jerome, opening in October.

The Granada War Relocation Center housed more than 7,000 Japanese Americans.

MILTON EISENHOWER

Milton Eisenhower served as director of information at the U.S. Department of Agriculture from 1928 to 1941. He was the brother of General Dwight D. Eisenhower, who later commanded the Allied forces in Europe and was elected U.S. president in 1952.

Milton Eisenhower was opposed to large-scale internment of Japanese Americans. He wanted to let women and children stay in their homes on the West Coast. As head of the War Relocation Authority, he worked to improve camp conditions for the internees. He helped establish an advisory council made up of Japanese Americans, as well as programs that allowed some internees to leave the camps to work on farms or finish their college educations. But the government didn't use some of his ideas, such as having the government protect internees' interests in the property they had owned before they were placed in custody.

Unhappy with the government's direction for running the camps, Eisenhower quit his job at the WRA after just 90 days. He took a job as associate director of the Office of War Information. He later served as president of Kansas State University, Pennsylvania State University, and Johns Hopkins University.

Of the 120,000 Japanese people that were sent to relocation centers, half of them were children.

CHAPTER SIX

LIFE BEHIND BARBED WIRE

When the permanent camps opened, internees again packed their personal belongings and boarded buses or trains to travel from the assembly centers to the camps—now called relocation centers. The transfer of internees began in March 1942 and continued until mid-October.

Twenty-one-year-old Miné Okubo and her family had spent several months at the Tanforan assembly center when they boarded a train bound for Topaz, Utah. "The trip was a nightmare that lasted two nights and a day," she remembered later. "The first night was a novelty after four and a half months of internment. However, I could not sleep. . . . Many became train sick and vomited . . . [and] at one point on the way, a brick was thrown into one of the cars."

Upon arriving at the camps, the internees saw their new homes—simple wooden barracks surrounded by barbed wire. Outside the camps, armed soldiers patrolled the grounds. Inside, security guards carrying guns watched over the internees.

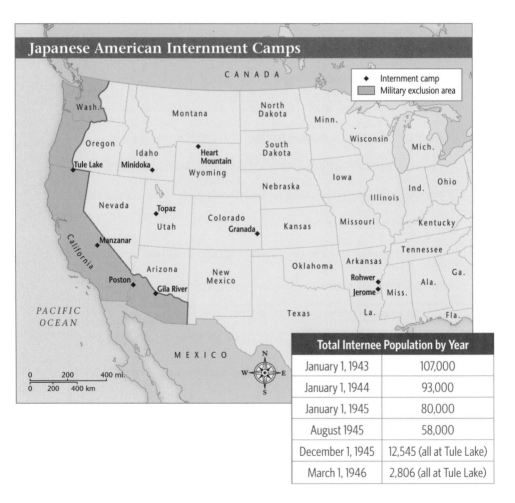

Japanese American Internment Camps

Total Internee Population by Year	
January 1, 1943	107,000
January 1, 1944	93,000
January 1, 1945	80,000
August 1945	58,000
December 1, 1945	12,545 (all at Tule Lake)
March 1, 1946	2,806 (all at Tule Lake)

THE CAMPS

Name	State	Opening Date	Closing Date	Peak Population
Gila River	Arizona	7/20/42	11/10/45	13,348
Granada	Colorado	8/24/42	10/15/45	7,318
Heart Mountain	Wyoming	8/12/42	11/10/45	10,767
Jerome	Arkansas	10/6/42	6/30/44	8,497
Manzanar	California	3/21/42	11/21/45	10,046
Minidoka	Idaho	8/10/42	10/28/45	9,397
Poston	Arizona	5/8/42	11/28/45	17,814
Rohwer	Arkansas	9/18/42	11/30/45	8,475
Topaz	Utah	9/11/42	10/31/45	8,130
Tule Lake	California	5/27/42	3/20/46	18,789

Education Resources. CLPEF Network. http://www.momomedia.com/CLPEF/camps.html

Most of the internees were accustomed to the mild
temperatures of the West Coast. At the mountain
camps in Idaho, Wyoming, and Colorado, winter
temperatures could reach minus 30 degrees Fahrenheit
(minus 34 degrees Celsius). At the desert camps in
Arizona, summer temperatures often soared above
100 degrees F (38 degrees C). Few internees had brought
clothing that was suitable for their new climate. At
Manzanar, they were issued military surplus clothing left
over from World War I, including coats, caps, and pants.

"I couldn't help laughing at Mama walking around in Army earmuffs and a pair of wide-cuffed, khaki-colored trousers several sizes too big for her," Jeanne Wakatsuki later remembered. Later the government sent sewing machines to the camp, so internees could alter the clothing to fit themselves.

Entire families lived in spaces 20 feet (6 meters) wide and from 8 to 24 feet (2.4 to 7.3 m) long. The walls of the living spaces didn't reach the ceilings, so sounds and smells wafted from one space to another. Contagious diseases such as influenza, dysentery, and tuberculosis spread through the camps.

The detainees tried to make the best out of their cramped living conditions.

None of the living spaces had running water. Just as at the assembly centers, the internees had to use community latrines and showers. Besides providing no privacy, the latrines contributed to the spread of illness through poor sanitation. The overworked toilets often overflowed, spreading human waste over the floor. The food made people sick sometimes because it could spoil in the warm weather, and it was very different from what internees had eaten at home. The water for drinking and bathing was sometimes unclean. Metal was in short supply, so the camps used recycled oil pipes that left an oily residue in the water. Manzanar Relocation Center used untreated water from the Sierra Nevada. An internee, Dr. Yoshiye Togasaki, recognized the problem with the mountain water and urged the camp directors to put in a system that filtered and chlorinated the water. It then was safe to drink.

The internees did the best they could to deal with harsh living conditions and their loss of freedom. They used the tiny living spaces mostly as bedrooms and spent their waking hours in other places such as mess halls and other community areas. Many of the adults held jobs. The camps had their own farms and hospitals, and some workers cleaned, cooked, and sewed for other internees. Wages were very low, starting at $8 per month for unskilled laborers. The most highly skilled workers, such as doctors, earned only about $19 per month, which was much less than what they were paid before the war.

More than half of the internees were children. Each camp had elementary and high schools staffed by internees as well as teachers from the outside. But the

schools weren't equal to the schools the children had attended before going to the camps. The classrooms were crowded, with as many as 40 to 50 students being taught by one teacher. Sometimes it was easier to hold classes outside, especially during warm months. The schools

Because of a lack of space, classes were often held outdoors next to the barracks.

also suffered from shortages of supplies and equipment. But even with the tough conditions, students did their best to learn.

The camp authorities tried to provide ways for internees to enjoy their leisure time. They had their own libraries and newspapers, although government officials reviewed the articles before they were printed. They also had movie theaters, school dances, and organized teams for sports such as baseball, football, and softball. They attended religious services and celebrated holidays and other special events.

POSSIBLE BENEFITS

Some historians believe the camp experience may have benefited some Japanese Americans. If they had stayed where they were, prejudice might have kept them from holding certain jobs, and students might have been kept off sports teams. In the camps, adults could hold important jobs and serve as leaders, and students could play sports or pursue other interests.

But nothing could change the fact that they lost their freedom and that their internment took away the legal rights they held under the U.S. Constitution. Most of those who were interned had no idea when they would be released from the camps or what they would find when they returned home.

Mealtimes at the relocation centers were far from what a Japanese family traditionally enjoyed at home. Hundreds of people ate together in large mess halls.

Japanese Americans traditionally had close-knit families. Parents and grandparents were highly respected by the children and grandchildren, who were expected to follow their elders' rules. The camps changed the structure of many families. Instead of eating home-cooked meals together, family members ate at the mess halls according to the demands of work and school schedules. Schoolchildren often sat at tables with their friends instead of their family members. Also, as so-called enemy aliens, Issei were no longer allowed to make decisions for their families. Their Nisei children took over that role. Camp life also encouraged many Nisei to become more Americanized and reject Japanese traditions. This change was especially upsetting to Issei men, who were accustomed to being the heads of their families.

But not all internees remained at the camps. With so many American men serving as soldiers, farmers were needed to raise and harvest crops. Beginning in May 1942, a few internees left an Oregon assembly center to work on a nearby farm. They lived in a government-run camp that did not have barbed wire or guards. That year about 10,000 people were allowed to leave the camps to work on farms. Most had to return to the camps after the harvest, but a few were allowed to remain on the farms. During 1942 some Nisei college students also received permission to finish their studies at nearby colleges.

Young Nisei men had another way out of the camps. Before the attack on Pearl Harbor, about 3,000 Nisei had been drafted into the U.S. military. Others had volunteered to serve. But after the war started, the military discharged some of these soldiers because of concerns about their loyalty. The government also refused to let any more Japanese Americans enlist, even though there was no evidence that any Japanese American soldiers had been disloyal.

Military leaders changed their minds when they realized they needed people who were fluent in Japanese to translate enemy documents and radio messages and to question prisoners of war. The War Department began recruiting volunteers from the internment camps in mid-1942. At first they wanted Kibei—Nisei who had spent time studying in Japan. Then they broadened their search to include any Nisei who could speak even the most basic Japanese. About 6,000 internees went to learn Japanese at the Military Intelligence Service Language School at Camp Savage or Fort Snelling, both in Minnesota. Most of these soldiers served in noncombat jobs in Asia. But some saw military action, and nine were killed in battle.

Some federal government officials, including Milton Eisenhower and Assistant Secretary of War John McCloy, urged the military in 1942 to allow Japanese Americans

U.S. Army interpreters served in the Military Intelligence Service.

to volunteer for combat. Some military leaders opposed the plan, but in January 1943, President Roosevelt agreed that Nisei who could pass a written loyalty test would be allowed to join the U.S. Army. The test asked volunteers about their loyalty to the United States and their feelings about Japan. Army officials and FBI agents also questioned the volunteers before they were cleared to serve.

More than 1,000 Nisei passed the loyalty test, left the internment camps, and joined the 442nd Regimental Combat Team. Nisei from Hawaii also volunteered, and many of them served in the 100th Infantry Battalion, which merged into the 442nd Regiment in 1944. The regiment's motto was "Go for broke," meaning that the troops would do whatever they had to do to defeat the enemy. The first Japanese American soldiers saw combat action in September 1943. The regiment fought in Italy, France, and Germany, and almost one-third of the men were killed or wounded. It became

The 442nd Regiment earned more than 18,000 awards in less than two years in combat.

the most-decorated unit of its size and length of service in U.S. military history.

The 442nd's record proved that many Japanese Americans were loyal citizens. The government decided to give the loyalty test to all internees age 17 and older to see whether they could be trusted to leave the camps to work. The loyalty test would also be used to resettle some internees. Roosevelt and his advisers decided that some Japanese Americans would be allowed to leave the camps to live in cities far from the West Coast.

Two questions on the loyalty test upset many internees, however. Question 27 asked, "Are you willing to serve in the armed forces of the United States on combat duty, wherever ordered?" Question 28 asked whether the Japanese Americans would "swear unqualified allegiance to the United States" and end all "allegiance or obedience to the Japanese emperor, or any other foreign government, power, or organization."

Both Nisei and Issei were upset about the questions, but for different reasons. Regarding the first question, some members of both groups felt they were being asked to risk their lives without any guarantee that their legal rights would be restored after they left the camps. The second question seemed to be asking the Issei to renounce their Japanese citizenship. Since they couldn't become American citizens, doing so would mean that they weren't citizens of any country. For the Nisei, question 28 seemed to suggest they had allegiance to Japan's emperor, when they considered themselves loyal Americans. They believed the government was considering them guilty until proven innocent.

The Japanese American Citizens League advised internees to answer "yes" to the questions, which most of them did. The ones who answered "no," for whatever reason, were labeled disloyal. Nicknamed "no-nos" and "no-no boys," they were sent to the Tule Lake camp, which already housed a number of internees considered disloyal. Most of the "loyal" residents of Tule Lake were sent to other camps, except for about 4,000 who preferred not to move again. By summer 1943, Tule Lake was the only camp for supposedly disloyal Japanese Americans and their families. It soon became the largest camp, with more than 18,000 people.

By 1944 many Japanese Americans were daily proving their loyalty by fighting bravely in the military and working hard at off-camp jobs that aided the U.S. war effort. But most of them still remained behind barbed wire.

TROUBLE AT TULE LAKE

The government built new fences and watchtowers and installed eight tanks to help keep order at Tule Lake. But that didn't stop the unrest.

A group of Tule Lake farm workers staged a strike in October 1943 for better working conditions. The strikers became angry when replacement Japanese American workers were brought in from other camps and given higher pay. The army used tear gas to break up a large crowd protesting the distribution of camp supplies to the replacement workers on November 1. For a time, the camp was under martial law. To some Americans who still distrusted the internees, the Tule Lake "riot" was proof they still couldn't be trusted. A government aide at first believed a false report saying that 500 armed internees had taken a civilian official prisoner.

Harold Ickes was opposed to internment camps. After the camps were closed he said, "We gave the fancy name of 'relocation centers' to these dust bowls, but they were concentration camps nonetheless."

CHAPTER SEVEN

OUTCRY AGAINST THE CAMPS

The Allies were almost ready to launch a major attack in Europe against Germany by spring 1944. In the Pacific, they had driven the Japanese from several islands they had captured. U.S. planes would later use those islands as bases for bombing raids on Japan. The American leaders increasingly felt that the Allies would win the war, and the concerns about Japanese Americans were fading.

Not all Americans supported the internment camps, but few of them spoke out publicly against them. Some of President Roosevelt's advisers believed the camps weren't necessary, since most Japanese Americans, both Issei and Nisei, were loyal to the United States. One of them was Secretary of the Interior Harold Ickes, whose department had taken control of the WRA in early 1944. Ickes and his aides began to call for ending the ban on Japanese Americans in the military areas of the West Coast.

But most people were more likely to express their support of their Japanese American neighbors and friends in quieter ways, such as offering to store their possessions or look after their property while they were gone.

SUPPORT FROM THE FIRST LADY

First Lady Eleanor Roosevelt wasn't pleased with President Roosevelt's decision to issue Executive Order 9066. But she kept her personal feelings to herself for quite a while, while supporting her husband's decision in public.

She did what she could to help the internees, however. A government order limited how much money enemy aliens could take out of their bank accounts.

Eleanor Roosevelt saw how hard this restriction made it for Issei and their families to live. Through her efforts, the government eventually let the Issei take out $100 each month from their accounts, the equivalent of about $1,300 today.

Roosevelt visited the Gila River camp in Arizona in April 1943. She was shocked by the conditions that the internees were forced to live in, although she noted that they were

One group that did speak out was the American Civil Liberties Union (ACLU). The organization defends Americans' legal and constitutional rights. In 1942, soon after Roosevelt issued Executive Order 9066, the ACLU said giving the military the power to exclude citizens and aliens from certain zones could lead to "the most serious violation of civil rights since the war began."

Eleanor Roosevelt visited the Gila River camp on April 23, 1943.

making the best of the situation by growing their own food, attending school, and working to make their quarters more comfortable. In a speech, she recommended closing the camps as soon as possible. "To undo a mistake is always harder than not to create one originally," she said, "but we seldom have the foresight. Therefore we have no choice but to try to correct our past mistakes, and I hope that the recommendations of the staff of the War Relocation Authority, who have come to know individually most of the Japanese Americans in these various camps, will be accepted."

73

DRAFTING INTERNEES

The U.S. military in January 1944 began drafting Nisei men who had passed the loyalty test, even if they were still in the camps. Both the ACLU and JACL thought Nisei internees had a legal duty to obey the draft orders, and most of them did. But some young men refused to enter the military, reasoning that if the Japanese Americans could fight for the United States, they should be allowed to live freely in it.

The largest protest was at Heart Mountain, Wyoming, where 85 young men refused to leave the camp for military service. They and other protesters were arrested and jailed. The JACL apologized to the resisters in 2000 for not supporting their efforts to protest internment.

The ACLU said the only way the order would be fair would be to place all citizens—including Caucasians—in the zones under martial law or hold hearings for individual Japanese Americans so they could prove their loyalty.

ACLU leaders knew that it would be difficult to challenge the president's executive order outright. Instead, they decided to challenge some of the military's actions involved in carrying out the order. The ACLU soon became involved in two important legal cases related to the relocation.

The first case involved a curfew on enemy aliens,

including the Issei and
Nisei, that had been
issued in Military Area
#1—the western regions
of California, Arizona,
Washington, and
Oregon. It took effect
March 27, 1942, before
most Japanese Americans
left for the assembly
centers. The curfew
forbade Japanese

TO THE GENTLEMEN OF 17 YEARS TO 38 YEARS OF AGE

As you know fellow Americans, at last they did recognize and realize that we are Americans. We are going to be drafted soon, just like an American outside enjoying the freedom and liberty. But, don't you think they should reconsider the steps that they had taken?

As we believe that Mr. Roosevelt's speech at the Congress was not merely an excuse to draft us to soldier's and die in vain, we are demanding the following as an American Citizen:

(1) Personal apology from Gen. DeWitt regarding his statement "Jap is Jap" and be expelled from his office. We also want apology from Major Bowron and Gov. Warren, and American Legion of Cal.

(2) Freedom, Rights and Privilege should not be denied in California, militarily, economically, and politically.

(3) Open the barb-wire and withdraw the Guard-duty of M.P.

(4) Such signs as "No Jap", "You Rat", "No Orientals or Colored admitted" and etc. which were familiar in California, must be taken down throughout the U.S.A.

(5) No discrimination upon the Japanese securing occupations.

(6) Every opportunity must be given to the Japanese soldier for advancement in the Air Corps, in the Army, and in the Marine Corps.

(7) Japanese soldier must be mixed with other Caucasian soldier to fight side by side.

VOICE OF NISEI

A handbill with a list of demands was posted at the Poston camp by an internee in February 1944, after the president reinstated the draft for Japanese Americans. Its purpose was to get the Japanese their rights back.

Americans from traveling
more than 20 miles (32 km) from their homes, except to
report to wartime civilian control offices, and from being
out of their homes after 8 p.m.

Twenty-three-year-old Gordon Hirabayashi was
a Nisei studying at the University of Washington. He
was also a Quaker, a member of a Protestant faith that
opposes all war and racism. Hirabayashi was arrested
in May 1942 for ignoring both the curfew and the order

to go to an assembly center. Hirabayashi deliberately disobeyed the curfew and the order because he believed the new rules were unconstitutional and needed to be judged by the courts.

Hirabayashi was sent to jail, where he remained, because posting bail would automatically allow him to be sent to an internment camp. In October a federal court found him guilty on both counts and sentenced him to three months in jail. Hirabayashi appealed his conviction to a federal appeals court. The court asked the U.S. Supreme Court for advice on points of law in the case, and the Supreme Court then decided to handle the appeal itself.

The Supreme Court decided Hirabayashi's case in June 1943, along with an appeal from Minoru Yasui, another Nisei convicted of violating a curfew. All nine justices agreed that the men were fairly tried and found guilty. The government, they said, had the power to impose a curfew that was limited to enemy aliens and the Nisei. But the court didn't directly address whether

Roosevelt had the power to issue Executive Order 9066 in the first place.

Justice Harlan Stone wrote the opinion in *Hirabayashi v. United States.* It said the government had no way of knowing whether the Nisei were loyal to the United States, and that it therefore could take broad measures against all of them.

In December 1944 the Supreme Court heard another case involving an evacuation order. In May 1942 the family of 22-year-old Fred Korematsu reported to the Tanforan Assembly Center, but Korematsu refused to go. He changed his name and had surgery on his eyes to make them look less Asian.

DIFFERENCE OF OPINION

The Supreme Court reached a unanimous decision in *Hirabayashi v. United States.* Justice Frank Murphy initially wanted to vote against the decision. But Justice Felix Frankfurter convinced him that the Court should reach a unanimous decision in such an important case. Murphy went along with the decision, but he wrote a separate statement, saying, "The broad guarantees of . . . the Constitution protecting essential liberties are [not] suspended by the mere existence of a state of war."

He claimed to be Mexican American. But he was quickly arrested, tried, convicted, and sent to an internment camp. In a 6–3 decision, the Supreme Court again affirmed that the government had the right to move the Nisei out of certain areas during wartime. But once again, it didn't directly rule on whether the government had the legal right to send Japanese Americans to internment camps.

The three justices who supported Korematsu were Robert Jackson, Frank Murphy, and Owen Roberts. Jackson said he would have released Korematsu immediately if he could. The cases of Korematsu and

The Supreme Court in 1943 included nine justices. Although they all intially agreed the Japanese Americans were treated fairly, some later changed their minds.

Hirabayashi show that the Supreme Court had more than one opportunity to strike down Executive Order 9066, but it didn't. Some of the justices, however, began to change their views on internment.

In another ruling the Supreme Court supported a Nisei. On December 18, 1944, the same day the Court ruled on *Korematsu v. United States*, it also ruled on *Ex Parte Mitsuye Endo* (On Behalf of Mitsuye Endo). When the Japanese attacked Pearl Harbor, 22-year-old Endo was working for the California Department of Motor Vehicles. Shortly after the war started, Endo and other state workers were fired because of their race. The JACL asked lawyer James Purcell of San Francisco to help the fired workers. Purcell decided to use Endo's firing as a test case.

Endo was already at the Tule Lake internment camp when Purcell filed a habeas corpus petition on her behalf on July 13, 1942. The Latin phrase means "you have the body." If a habeas corpus request is granted, the government must allow a person being held against his or her will to go to court to ask for freedom. Endo

THE FACE OF AN IMPORTANT CASE

Mitsuye Endo, whose lawsuit led to the closing of the internment camps, was born in 1920 in Sacramento, California, to Japanese immigrant parents. After high school she started working in a clerical position at the Department of Motor Vehicles. She was one of from 300 to 500 state employees to be fired from their jobs after the attack on Pearl Harbor. Sixty-three of the employees, including Endo, asked the JACL to help them challenge their firings.

James Purcell, the lawyer handling the employees' case, never met Endo. But he asked her to be the plaintiff in the case partly because she was so Americanized. She was a Christian, her brother served in the U.S. Army, she had never been to Japan, and she couldn't speak or read the Japanese language. Endo wasn't sure at first that she wanted to do it, but she eventually agreed. She said later, "I agreed to do it at that moment, because they said it's for the good of everybody, and so I said, well, if that's it, I'll go ahead and do it."

After the lawsuit helped free the Japanese Americans from the camps, Endo moved to Chicago, Illinois, where she married and raised a family. Endo didn't speak publicly about the case, and she gave only one interview about it, in 1984. She died in April 2006 at age 85.

claimed that she was a loyal U.S. citizen who had not broken any laws and was being held in the camps against her will. In July 1943 Judge Michael Roche dismissed Endo's petition without any explanation. Purcell appealed the dismissal to the 9th U.S. Circuit Court of Appeals, which sent the case to the Supreme Court instead of ruling on it. By this time Endo had been moved from Tule Lake to Topaz.

In a unanimous decision, the Supreme Court ruled that Endo was being held by the War Relocation Authority instead of the military. As a civilian organization, the WRA couldn't legally hold Endo once she was evacuated from the military areas and proved that she was not a threat to national security. The Court ordered that she be released from Topaz.

The decision in Endo's case applied to thousands of other Nisei who were loyal and posed no threat to the United States. The time of the internment camps was coming to an end.

The Jerome War Relocation Center was the first camp to close. Internees were transferred to one of four other camps, where they remained until the exclusion order was canceled and the Japanese Americans were allowed to return home.

CHAPTER EIGHT

CLOSING THE CAMPS

The Supreme Court decision in *Ex Parte Endo* was a partial victory for the internees. It meant that all Nisei who had passed the loyalty test were free to leave the camps and return to their homes. On December 17, 1944, the day before the Supreme Court's decision in the case was handed down, President Roosevelt issued Public Proclamation No. 21. It officially canceled the exclusion order and let the Nisei return to the West Coast beginning in January 1945. By then about 80,000 people were living in the camps, down from a peak of 107,000 in 1943.

Not all of the camps were still open. With fewer internees, the government needed fewer camps. The Nisei were happy to leave the camps behind, but many

were afraid of how they would be treated by their
Caucasian neighbors when they returned home. They
were also sad about having to leave their Issei relatives
and friends behind. But by the spring of 1945, the pace of
resettlement in California and the rest of the West Coast
had increased.

Franklin Roosevelt, the country's longest-serving
president, had been in poor health during the war years,
and he died of a cerebral hemorrhage on April 12, 1945.
Vice President Harry Truman became president. A few
weeks later, on May 7, 1945, Germany surrendered to the
Allies, ending the war in Europe. The Japanese, however,
continued to fight, even though they suffered a major
loss when the Allies defeated them on June 22 in the
82-day Battle of Okinawa.

President Truman knew that the war in the Pacific
needed to end as soon as possible. Scientists working
for the U.S. military had developed the most powerful
weapon ever produced, the atomic bomb. Although
Truman was deeply troubled by the idea of killing tens
of thousands of Japanese civilians, he believed that

The atomic bomb flattened nearly every building in Hiroshima and killed about 80,000 people in the first few seconds after the explosion.

bombing Japan would force its leaders to surrender, saving the Allies from launching a ground invasion.

On August 6 and 9, 1945, the United States dropped atomic bombs on the Japanese cities of Hiroshima and Nagasaki. Japanese Emperor Hirohito announced Japan's surrender on August 15. The surrender treaty was signed September 2 aboard the battleship USS *Missouri* in Tokyo Bay.

With the war ending, most of the remaining 44,000 Japanese American internees knew they would soon be

FIRST-PERSON ACCOUNTS

Several former internees documented their experiences in books. They include artist and writer Miné Okubo's illustrated book *Citizen 13660*, which was published in 1946 and is believed to be the first book about the camps written by an internee. The title refers to the number that was assigned to the Okubo family in the camps. In 1973 Jeanne Wakatsuki Houston and her husband, James Houston, published *Farewell to Manzanar*, which was made into a TV movie in 1976. Yoshiko Uchida wrote about her experiences in several children's books, including *Desert Exile* and *Journey to Topaz*.

going home. U.S. officials had already told camp leaders that the camps would be closed within a year of the war's end. Actually, all of the camps except Tule Lake were closed by the end of 1945.

After years of internment, Japanese Americans didn't know what awaited them as they returned to life on the outside. Many looked to the WRA for help, asking for loans or other aid so they could replace the items that had been stolen or that they had sold, usually at a great loss, before leaving for the camps. The government refused. Instead it gave each family $50 (worth about

$650 today) and train tickets to the location from which they had traveled to reach the camps. Many Japanese Americans knew that their farms, homes, and businesses were gone, so they tried to stay in the camps as long as they could. The government eventually packed their belongings for them and forced them to leave.

Tule Lake, which held the so-called disloyal Japanese Americans, was the last to close. All remaining internees left in March 1946. About 5,000 of the internees at Tule Lake decided to move to Japan instead of returning to their homes on the West Coast. Many were Nisei who felt betrayed by the United States because of what they had been forced to endure during the war. They chose to give up their U.S. citizenship.

The rest of the Japanese Americans prepared to return to their homes. They knew that their lives were forever changed, but not how much.

DEATHS IN THE CAMPS

Seven camp internees were shot and killed by guards, either during escape attempts or protests. Poor living conditions and lack of adequate health care contributed to the deaths of others in the camps.

Fred Korematsu (from left), Minoru Yasui, and Gordon Hirabayashi filed petitions in 1983 asking to have their cases reopened.

CHAPTER NINE

BACK TO SOCIETY

The Japanese Americans who returned to the West Coast found life outside the camps almost as difficult for them as it had been inside. Their lives and status before the war were gone. Many farmers had lost their farms and farm equipment. Fishermen no longer had their boats, and business owners found their businesses looted and vandalized or being run by Caucasian owners. The possessions that many internees had stored in warehouses for safekeeping had been stolen.

Some Japanese Americans were treated with prejudice and violence when they returned. People on the street would shout at them to go to Japan. Children were sometimes bullied in school, and Japanese homes and places of worship were vandalized or sometimes burned. Housing, which was scarce for everyone after World War II, was especially hard for Japanese American families to find.

Jeanne Wakatsuki and her family moved into a three-bedroom apartment in Long Beach, California. At last, they had a kitchen and an indoor bathroom. But the breakdown in family life that had begun in the camps continued after the family's release. Jeanne's father, Ko, failed in several attempts to start a business, and he began abusing alcohol. Her mother went to work in a cannery to support the family.

Jeanne did well in school and made friends, but some children in her class weren't allowed to play with her because she was Japanese. The leader of a Girl Scout troop refused to let her join. When she tried out for a place in her high school band as a majorette, the school board had to debate the issue. "When they finally assented, I was grateful . . . [and] even if my once enviable role now seemed vaguely second-rate, I was determined to try twice as hard to prove they'd made the right choice," she said later.

President Truman wanted to help the former internees. He asked Congress in 1948 to pass the Japanese American Claims Act. This law was intended to repay the internees for some of the property they had lost before evacuation. The law was amended in 1956 to limit the amount of a single claim to $100,000. At times the government fought claims for payment. Internees were compensated for only about 10 percent of the value of the property they had lost.

Congress passed another law in 1952 that affected Japanese Americans. The Immigration and Nationality Act, also called the McCarran-Walter Act, ended the restrictions on

RESETTLEMENT CITIES

Starting in 1943, several U.S. cities welcomed internees who were allowed to leave the camps but were still banned from living on the West Coast. Some former internees moved to Colorado, Utah, and Idaho, while others moved farther east. The largest number—approximately 8,000—had settled in Illinois, mostly in Chicago, by November 1944. Many other released internees moved to Cincinnati, Ohio. Both cities offered jobs, as well as less prejudice than Japanese Americans encountered in western states.

JAPANESE AMERICAN INTERNMENT

Japanese immigration in place since 1924. The law also said that Issei and new Japanese immigrants could become naturalized U.S. citizens. But the law preserved immigration quotas, except that now they were based on race instead of country of origin. For example, a person born in Denmark to a Japanese father and a Danish mother would be counted in the immigration quotas for Japan, instead of Denmark. President Truman vetoed the bill, but Congress overrode his veto, and the bill became law.

For the next few decades, many former internees quietly rebuilt their lives and tried to show that they were loyal Americans. But some still felt bitter over how they had been treated. Members of the JACL asked the U.S. government in 1970 to pay reparations. The money would go to anyone who had been in the camps, and it would partly compensate them for the financial, physical, and emotional injuries they had suffered. But it took years for the payments to be approved.

Not until 1976 was Executive Order 9066 repealed. It was the nation's bicentennial—the 200th anniversary of

PRESIDENT TRUMAN

The treatment that the returning internees received angered President Harry Truman, who believed the camps should not have been used. Years after leaving the White House, he told a writer: "They were concentration camps. They called it relocation, but they put them in concentration camps, and I was against it. We were in a period of emergency, but it was still the wrong thing to do. It was one place where I never went along with [President] Roosevelt. He never should have allowed it. . . . People out on the West Coast got scared, and they panicked, and they decided to get rid of the Japanese Americans. . . . What a leader has to do is stop the panic."

In 1946 Truman tried to show his admiration for how Japanese Americans dealt with their wartime experience. He invited members of the 442nd Regiment to the White House. "You fought not only the enemy," Truman said to the soldiers, "but you fought prejudice—and you have won."

President Truman visited with the soldiers in the 442nd Regiment in July 1946.

THE CAMPS TODAY

After the war, most of the buildings at the internment camps were torn down or moved to other sites. The land was either sold back to the previous owners or turned over to U.S. government agencies. Over the years, the buildings left behind at the camps began to fall apart.

Today the Manzanar camp is the only one with buildings still standing. A few, including the armory, are the original buildings, but the rest were rebuilt by the National Park Service. Manzanar is a National Historic Site, with exhibits and a film explaining the relocation process during World War II. The government lists six of the 10 camps as historically important places. Signs and monuments at the camps contain information for visitors about the internment.

More than a million people have visited the Manzanar National Historic Site.

the founding of the United States. President Gerald Ford said that although the country had much to celebrate, it should also remember its national mistakes. "We now know," Ford said of the internment program, "what we should have known then—not only was that evacuation wrong, but Japanese Americans were and are loyal Americans. . . . I call upon the American people to affirm with me this American Promise—that we have learned from the tragedy of that long-ago experience forever to treasure liberty and justice for each individual American, and resolve that this kind of action shall never be repeated again."

A Commission on Wartime Relocation and Internment of Civilians (CWRIC) was formed in 1980 to investigate the treatment of Japanese Americans during World War II. It held hearings in cities across the United States, seeking information from former internees. Almost two years later, the commission issued its report to Congress. It said President Roosevelt's decision to intern the Japanese Americans "followed a long and ugly history of West Coast anti-Japanese agitation and legislation." The report included some former internees' recollections of life in the camps.

CWRIC recommended in 1983 that the U.S. government pay $20,000 to each living internee. That same year Fred Korematsu and Gordon Hirabayashi challenged the decisions made in their wartime legal battles. Minori Yasui, who also had brought a case challenging internment to the Supreme Court during the war, joined them. Yasui died in 1986 while the case was still under review.

Korematsu and Hirabayashi learned that government officials had lied or withheld evidence during their wartime legal cases. The Supreme Court had ruled against Korematsu and the others based on the false and missing evidence. The men presented their evidence to a federal court, hoping that the earlier decisions would be reversed. Korematsu believed that if his wartime conviction was allowed to stand, other Americans guilty of nothing could someday be held in prison or concentration camps without a trial or a hearing.

In the end, both men won their arguments, and their original convictions were overturned— Korematsu's in 1984 and Hirabayashi's in 1987. Both men also received the highest honor an American civilian can receive, the Presidential Medal of Freedom. In 1998 President Bill Clinton presented Korematsu, who died in

President Clinton presented Fred Korematsu with the Presidential Medal of Freedom on January 15, 1998.

2005, with the medal. Hirabayashi, who died in January 2012, received the Medal of Freedom posthumously in April 2012. President Barack Obama presented it to his family.

After Hirabayashi's conviction was overturned, Congress took action on the CWRIC report. In 1988 Congress agreed to give each internee a reparation payment of $20,000. At that time about 60,000 internees

The first reparation payments were presented to Kisa Isari (from left), Hau Dairiki, and Mamoru Eto on October 9, 1990.

were still alive. The first payment, made in 1990 under President George H.W. Bush, went to the oldest surviving internee, 107-year-old Mamoru Eto. Along with the check came a written apology. Former internee Suyako Kitashima attended the ceremony. "I just broke down," she later said. "[For] many old people, the mere fact that the president apologized is what they were living for."

In the letter to the internees, President George H.W. Bush offered the nation's "sincere apology," and said,

"A monetary sum and words alone cannot restore lost years or erase painful memories; neither can they fully convey our Nation's resolve to rectify injustice and to uphold the rights of individuals. We can never fully right the wrongs of the past. But we can take a clear stand for justice and recognize that serious injustices were done to Japanese Americans during World War II."

The reparation payments, which totaled $1.6 billion, continued until 1999. Although the U.S. government and the courts finally admitted that internment had been a mistake, the admission came too late for the many internees who had died in the meantime.

The Japanese American experience during World War II still has a powerful impact on the lives of the surviving internees and their families. And it reminds all Americans that protecting civil liberties is a constant struggle, especially during a time of war.

TIMELINE

▶ **February 1907**
President Theodore Roosevelt begins working on the Gentleman's Agreement, which limits the number of Japanese immigrants allowed to enter the country

▶ **May 6, 1924**
President Calvin Coolidge signs into law a bill that ends almost all immigration from Japan

▶ **September 1, 1939**
Germany invades Poland, starting World War II

▶ **September 27, 1940**
Japan, Italy, and Germany form the Axis Alliance to fight against the Allies

▶ **December 7, 1941**
Japan launches a surprise attack on the U.S. Navy base at Pearl Harbor, Hawaii; the U.S. government begins arresting Japanese Americans considered dangerous enemy aliens

▶ **December 8, 1941**
The United States declares war on Japan and enters World War II as part of the Allies

▶ **February 19, 1942**
President Roosevelt issues Executive Order 9066, which gives the military the power to remove anyone from parts of the country called military areas

▶ **March 2, 1942**
General John DeWitt declares California and parts of three other states as Military Area 1; the first evacuations to assembly centers begin later in the month

▶ **March 21, 1942**
The first relocation camp, Manzanar, opens in California

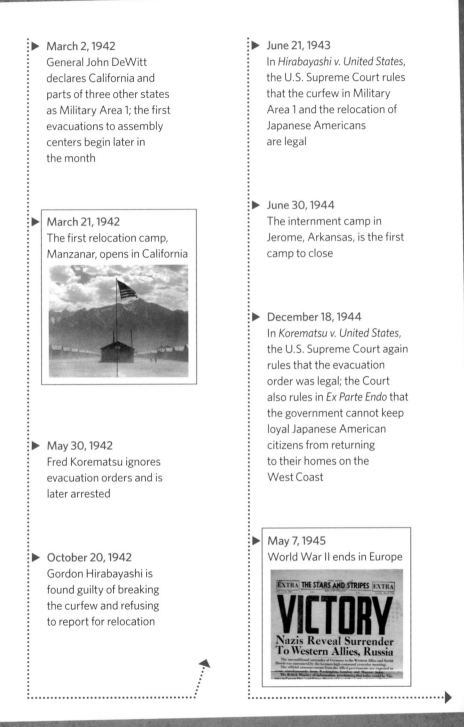

▶ **May 30, 1942**
Fred Korematsu ignores evacuation orders and is later arrested

▶ **October 20, 1942**
Gordon Hirabayashi is found guilty of breaking the curfew and refusing to report for relocation

▶ **June 21, 1943**
In *Hirabayashi v. United States*, the U.S. Supreme Court rules that the curfew in Military Area 1 and the relocation of Japanese Americans are legal

▶ **June 30, 1944**
The internment camp in Jerome, Arkansas, is the first camp to close

▶ **December 18, 1944**
In *Korematsu v. United States*, the U.S. Supreme Court again rules that the evacuation order was legal; the Court also rules in *Ex Parte Endo* that the government cannot keep loyal Japanese American citizens from returning to their homes on the West Coast

▶ **May 7, 1945**
World War II ends in Europe

EXTRA **THE STARS AND STRIPES** EXTRA

VICTORY

Nazis Reveal Surrender To Western Allies, Russia

The unconditional surrender of Germany to the Western Allies and Soviet Russia was announced by the Germans high command yesterday morning.

The official announcements from the Allied governments are expected to be made today.

The British Ministry of Information, proclaiming that today would be V-

August 6, 1945
The U.S. military drops an atomic bomb on Hiroshima, Japan; the U.S. military drops an atomic bomb on Nagasaki, Japan, three days later

August 14, 1945
Japan's Emperor Hirohito agrees to surrender to the Allies; the war officially ends in September

March 20, 1946
The internment camp in Tule Lake, California, is the last camp to close

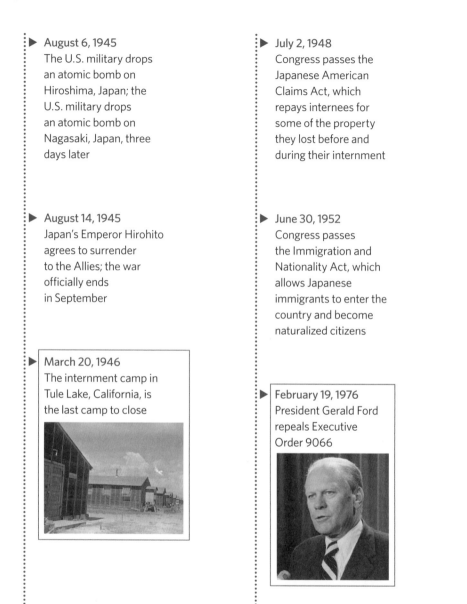

July 2, 1948
Congress passes the Japanese American Claims Act, which repays internees for some of the property they lost before and during their internment

June 30, 1952
Congress passes the Immigration and Nationality Act, which allows Japanese immigrants to enter the country and become naturalized citizens

February 19, 1976
President Gerald Ford repeals Executive Order 9066

▶ June 16, 1983
Commission on
Wartime Relocation and
Internment of Civilians
recommends that
Congress give each living
internee $20,000

▶ July 14, 1984
A federal court overturns
Fred Korematsu's
conviction

▶ September 24, 1987
A federal court overturns
Gordon Hirabayashi's
conviction

▶ 1990
The U.S. government
makes its first reparation
payments to Japanese
internees

▶ January 15, 1998
President Bill Clinton
awards Fred Korematsu
the Presidential Medal
of Freedom

▶ April 26, 2012
President Barack
Obama awards Gordon
Hirabayashi the
Presidential Medal of
Freedom posthumously

▶ November 24, 2015
President Barack Obama
awards Minoru Yasui the
Presidential Medal of
Freedom posthumously

GLOSSARY

alien—citizen of a country who lives in another country

allies—people or countries united for a common purpose; when capitalized, refers to the United States and its allies during major wars

civil rights— the rights that all people have to freedom and equal treatment under the law

civilian—person who is not in the military

discrimination— unfair treatment of a person or group, often because of race, religion, gender, sexual preference, or age

draft—system that chooses people who are compelled by law to serve in the military

espionage—spying

evacuate—to remove people from an area, often to escape danger

internment—the confinement under guard of an enemy or suspicious person

naturalize—to become a citizen of a country or state although born in another country

plaintiff—person or group of people who file the complaint in a lawsuit

prejudice—hatred or unfair treatment of a group of people who belong to a certain social category, such as race or religion

racism—belief that one race is better than another

reparations—payments made to compensate for wrongdoing

repeal—to cancel a law

sabotage—to damage, destroy, or interfere with on purpose

FURTHER READING

Bjorklund, Ruth. *Japanese Americans in World War II.*
New York: Cavendish Square Publishing, 2017.

Marrin, Albert. *Uprooted: The Japanese American Experience During World War II.* New York: Alfred A. Knopf, 2016.

Taylor, Charlotte, and Deborah Kent. *The Internment of Japanese Americans.* New York: Enslow Publishing, 2016.

Welky, Ali, ed. *A Captive Audience: Voices of Japanese American Youth in World War II Arkansas.* Little Rock, Ark.: Butler Center Books, 2015.

INTERNET SITES

Use FactHound to find Internet sites related to this book.

Visit *www.facthound.com*
Just type in 9780756555818 and go.

CRITICAL THINKING QUESTIONS

U.S. leaders were debating issues about immigration in 2016 and 2017. Do you see any similarities between the situation today and the situation facing the Japanese in the 1940s? Support your answer with evidence from the text.

Imagine you were living in the United States during World War II. Would you have approved of the idea of moving the Japanese to internment camps? Why or why not?

Did the reparations given to Japanese Americans in the 1990s make up for what they experienced during the war? Support your answer with evidence from the text.

SOURCE NOTES

Page 22, line 8: John Tateishi. *And Justice for All: An Oral History of the Japanese American Detention Camps*. New York: Random House, 1984, p. 5.

Page 26, line 9: Robert Dallek. *Franklin D. Roosevelt and American Foreign Policy, 1932–1945*. New York: Oxford University Press, 1979, p. 75.

Page 27, col. 2, line 1: Greg Robinson. *By Order of the President: FDR and the Internment of Japanese Americans*. Cambridge, Mass.: Harvard University Press, 2001, p. 66.

Page 30, line 15: David Colbert, ed. *Eyewitness to America: 500 years of America In The Words Of Those Who Saw It Happen*. New York: Pantheon Books, 1997, p. 400.

Page 35, line 12: Roger Daniels. *Prisoners Without Trial: Japanese Americans in World War II*. Rev. ed. New York: Hill and Wang, 2004, p. 35.

Page 36, line 9: *By Order of the President: FDR and the Internment of Japanese Americans*, p. 75.

Page 37, col. 2, line 3: *Prisoners Without Trial: Japanese Americans in World War II*, p. 49.

Page 38, line 7: "Chronology of 1942 San Francisco War Events." Virtual Museum of the City of San Francisco. 17 Jan. 2017. www.sfmuseum.org/war/42.html

Page 40, line 1: *Prisoners Without Trial: Japanese Americans in World War II*, p. 145.

Page 41, col. 2, line 9: Jeanne Wakatsuki Houston and James D. Houston. *Farewell to Manzanar: A True Story of Japanese American Experience During and After the World War II Internment*. Boston: Houghton Mifflin, 1973, p. 13.

Page 44, line 19: Richard L. Miller. "Confiscations from Japanese-Americans During World War II." Forfeiture Endangers American Rights. 6 Nov. 2001. 17 Jan. 2017. http://www.fear.org/RMillerJ-A.html

Page 45, line 18: David Mas Masumoto. "A Bitter Harvest: Inside Japanese-American Internment Camps During World War II." *Modern Farmer*. 13 Oct. 2015. 17 Jan. 2017. http://modernfarmer.com/2015/10/japanese-american-internment-camps/

Page 48, col. 1, line 8: David K. Yoo. *Growing up Nisei: Race, Generation, and Culture Among Japanese Americans of California, 1924–49*. Urbana: University of Illinois Press, 2000, p. 145.

Page 49, line 9: Lawson Fusao Inada, ed. *Only What We Could Carry: The Japanese American Internment Experience*. Berkeley, Calif.: Heyday Books, 2000, p. 70.

Page 50, line 17: Ibid., p. 75.

Page 55, line 9: Ibid., p. 93.

Page 58, line 1: *Farewell to Manzanar: A True Story of Japanese American Experience During and After the World War II Internment*, p. 26.

Page 67, line 12: Statement of United States Citizen of Japanese Ancestry. 17 Jan. 2017. http://encyclopedia.densho.org/media/encyc-psms/en-denshopd-p72-00004-3.pdf

Page 73, line 6: R. Jeffrey Blair. "In Opposition to the Japanese Internment: The ACLU During World War II." Aichi Gakuin University. 17 Jan. 2017. www.aichi-gakuin.ac.jp/~jeffreyb/research/ACLU.one.TextB.html#oppol

Page 73, col. 1, line 6: "Eleanor Roosevelt: Undo the Mistake of Internment." National Park Service. 17 Jan. 2017. https://www.nps.gov/articles/erooseveltinternment.htm

Page 77, col. 1, line 11: Peter Irons, ed. *Justice Delayed: The Record of the Japanese American Internment Cases*. Middletown, Conn.: Wesleyan University Press, 1989, p. 68.

Page 80, col. 2, line 6: Brian Niiya. "Mitsuye Endo: The Woman Behind the Landmark Supreme Court Case." Densho Blog. 24 March 2016. 17 Jan. 2017. http://www.densho.org/mitsuye-endo/

Page 90, line 17: *Farewell to Manzanar: A True Story of Japanese American Experience During and After the World War II Internment*, p. 153.

Page 93, col. 1, line 6: Merle Miller. *Plain Speaking: An Oral Biography of Harry S. Truman*. New York: Berkley Pub. Corp., 1974, pp. 421–422.

Page 93, col. 2, line 8: *By Order of the President: FDR and the Internment of Japanese Americans*, p. 258.

Page 95, line 3: "Ford Proclamation: An American Promise." 19 Feb. 1976. 17 Jan. 2017. A More Perfect Union. National Museum of American History. http://amhistory.si.edu/perfectunion/collection/image.asp?ID=1281

Page 95, line 20: *Justice Delayed: The Record of the Japanese American Internment Cases*, p. 106.

Page 98, line 5: Ibid., p. 243.

Page 99, line 1: "Letter from George H.W. Bush to Japanese Americans." Alliance Community Collections. 31 Jan. 2017. https://ccacommunitycollections.omeka.net/items/show/437

SELECT BIBLIOGRAPHY

Burton, Jeffrey F., et al. *Confinement and Ethnicity: An Overview of World War II Japanese American Relocation Sites*. Seattle: University of Washington Press, 2002.

Colbert, David, ed. *Eyewitness to America: 500 Years of America in the Words of Those Who Saw It Happen*. New York: Pantheon Books, 1997.

Dallek, Robert. *Franklin D. Roosevelt and American Foreign Policy, 1932–1945*. New York: Oxford University Press, 1979.

Daniels, Roger. *Prisoners Without Trial: Japanese Americans in World War II*. Rev. ed. New York: Hill and Wang, 2004.

Daniels, Roger, Sandra C. Taylor, and Harry H. L. Kitano, eds. *Japanese Americans: From Relocation to Redress*. Rev. ed. Seattle: University of Washington Press, 1991.

Hansen, Arthur A., ed. *Japanese American World War II Evacuation Oral History Project. Part IV: Resisters*. Munich, Germany: K.G. Saur, 1995.

Houston, Jeanne Wakatsuki, and James D. Houston. *Farewell to Manzanar: A True Story of Japanese American Experience During and After the World War II Internment*. Boston: Houghton Mifflin, 1973.

Inada, Lawson Fusao, ed. *Only What We Could Carry: The Japanese American Internment Experience*. Berkeley, Calif.: Heyday Books, 2000.

Irons, Peter, ed. *Justice Delayed: The Record of the Japanese American Internment Cases*. Middletown, Conn.: Wesleyan University Press, 1989.

Japanese American Citizens League. https://jacl.org/about/

Miller, Merle. *Plain Speaking: An Oral Biography of Harry S. Truman*. New York: Berkley Pub. Corp., 1974.

Reeves, Richard. *Infamy: The Shocking Story of the Japanese American Interment in World War II*. New York: Henry Holt and Company, 2015.

Robinson, Greg. *By Order of the President: FDR and the Internment of Japanese Americans*. Cambridge, Mass.: Harvard University Press, 2001.

Tateishi, John. *And Justice for All: An Oral History of the Japanese American Detention Camps*. New York: Random House, 1984.

Yoo, David K. *Growing up Nisei: Race, Generation, and Culture Among Japanese Americans of California, 1924–49*. Urbana: University of Illinois Press, 2000.

INDEX